The Tyranny of Perfection:
Finding True Pleasure

Michael Demkovich

A Trilogy on Trust:
Learning to Love, Believe, and Hope Again

Desert Willow Project

Demkovich, Michael

   The Tyranny of Perfection: Finding True Pleasure. A Trilogy on Trust: Learning to Love, Believe, and Hope Again.

ISBN 978-1-7345410-0-7

   Spirituality. Catholic Philosophy. Theology.

"This is a liberating book. Never before had I faced how "the tyranny of perfection" can inhabit one's life like an incubus, constantly sowing dissatisfaction with how things are, how others are, how I am too! Demkovich shows how this inhibits our happy dwelling in this fractured and fragile world, with its beauty which shines forth even in imperfection, and its wholesome pleasures. The threefold disciplines of science, art and religion, pursuing truth, beauty and goodness, form us for that holiness which is not of our making but a gift. Trustingly we can be both at ease with each other and ourselves, and yet learn to be open to more than we can achieve by our own efforts, God's own self-gift. This book left me with a feeling of peace that has nothing to do with complacency. A refreshing drink in an oasis as one journeys."

Timothy Radcliffe, OP
Theologian, author, and former
Master of the Dominican Order

The first in a trilogy, *The Tyranny of Perfection* is a must-read for anyone who struggles with "the myth of perfection." Michael Demkovich skillfully weaves classic terms and tales on the theme of perfectionism into a beautifully written intellectual treatise on a very challenging topic.

Vanessa Guerin
Director of Publications and Events,
Center for Action and Contemplation

Table of contents

Preface

Trust is vital in so many dimension of our private and public life. But why? Well, it is first and foremost about believing. It is a primary attitude one person shows toward another. Before we even learn to understand, our first condition is that of vulnerability which demands trust. Every helpless infant must trust in the good of humanity. Trust, we learn, can be given to persons and things, to an individual or a community, to an ideal, or to an object. It indicates a sense of reliability that both fashions and upholds the relationship. It also names the truth of the relationship, a genuine honesty of things. It can also speak to us of the abilities of another person or of things as trustworthy.

It was during Lincoln's years as president, during the Civil War, a time of national division, when the U.S. Treasury of the Union decided to include the phrase "In God We Trust" on their currency. The original phrase had been "In God is Our Trust" but that was changed by Secretary of the Treasury Salmon P. Chase, and passed by an act of Congress in 1864. If I may be a bit pessimistic, perhaps today the U.S. currency might read "Trust No One." However, trust is *de facto* essential to the commerce of social life and to human happiness, so why have we become so suspicious?

That is the question this trilogy on trust explores. It raises for us the question of a kind of default suspicion in society, a trend to assume the negative. Each work in the trilogy will explore the sources of suspicion, the deep seated absolute distrust of all pleasure, wealth, and power regardless of virtuous or noble purpose. The philosophical genesis of this suspicion can be found in the thought of Sigmund Freud, Karl Marx, and Friedrich Nietzsche. Together they have been called the "Masters of Suspicion" by Paul Ricoeur for their negative presuppositions in all interpretation. And yet, trust is perhaps as critical to our environment as are clean air and clean water. A climate of trust is vital to human flourishing and skepticism is like a poison that destroys a community's ability to risk and to be vulnerable. We have seen a steady decline in the levels of trust. The Pew Research Center has been studying the question of trust in society for decades.[1] Alarmingly, 71% of adults believe Americans are less confident in each other than they were 20 years ago. "About three-in-four Americans (79%) think their fellow citizens have too little confidence in each other. Relatedly, a fifth of adults (21%) think personal confidence in the country has worsened for little good reason" (29). The question of distrust is alarming and we need to examine its harm and what will heal it.

In this work, *The Tyranny of Perfection*, we see how suspicion has robbed us of the simple delight of being. This Freudian fracturing and critical analysis of the person into id, ego, superego has left us unable to trust pleasure itself. This self-alienation denies that necessary wholeness of life. It compartmentalizes life and how we think about life. Freud is just one player in Modernity's abuse of science, casting it as superior to all other disciplines. Fragmentation

---

[1] https://www.people-press.org/2019/07/22/trust-and-distrust-in-america/ 8/14/2019

and specialization have alienated the disciplines of science, art, and religion. Rather than the three together providing the integration of life and living, science, art, and religion have wrongly been cast as opposed to each other. The tyranny is this undermining of the greatest pleasure, our ability to love life with all its fragile qualities. Wealth and power, we will see, also attack our sense of trust, but for now, we will look at the tragic loss of trust in pleasure.

The other two works in this trilogy, *The Want of Wealth* and *The Bondage of Power*, examine the seeds of suspicion that have led us to mistrust both economics and politics, both wealth and power. It is this widespread mistrust that has brought us to tragic levels of alienation and isolation, not pleasure, wealth, and power *per se*. These can be abused as tools of alienation, division and suspicion. As we will see in this trilogy, we must learn to love, to believe, and to hope again as our social corrective. If these three books help to initiate greater interest in our learning to trust once more, then they will have served a good and noble purpose.

Introduction

I was inspired to undertake this project, three works on trust, teaching us how to love, to believe, and to hope, because of the many people, young and old, who feel so lost, especially the young. In my work and ministry, I have seen time and time again the deep seated dynamic of self-alienation, of a paralyzing sense of inadequacy. I have observed that with millennials in particular, we have succeeded in creating a generation that outwardly seems so self-assured, but are inwardly so insecure. As true as this is, it is not limited to just the young. More and more I have found that given the tenor of public discourse with its cruel "social shaming," adults and even the elderly, are plagued by a self-doubt, a feeling that there is something wrong with life. This sad statement captures what I've heard a number of people express in different ways, "I'm sick and tired of all this anger and mistrust. I'd be happy to go home to God instead of having to put up with all of this." So my question is, "Why do we feel this way? How did we get to this point? Why is there so much mistrust?"

As I have visited with people in spiritual direction, or in counseling, or even in social gatherings, I have become more and more aware that one of the fundamental issues is perfection. The world isn't perfect! The Church isn't perfect! Our government isn't perfect! Society today isn't perfect! You're not perfect! Even I am not perfect! This myth of perfection has made it so difficult, even angering, for us to have to face the flawed reality of life. So what do we mean by perfection and how did it become so self-alienating?

Most people hear the word "perfection" as suggesting a kind of "excellence" or something that is "ideal" or that it indicates a sense of "accomplishment" and this is fine, if we are dealing with an existing reality, a done deal. However, the tyranny of perfection arises when we confuse fact for fantasy. The Army slogan from the 1990's, "Be All You Can Be" says one thing but "you're no good" or "you'll never amount to anything" says another. The first acknowledges a process of becoming the second ends in stagnant pessimistic condemnation. On the one hand, perfection is about a reality that is or was, which is a declarative sentence, *"The weather that day was perfect,"* it states a fact – "you did you're best." On the other hand, when we think of perfection as an imperative sentence, *"The weather must be perfect"* it commands and imposes an unrealistic standard – "you must be perfect." Here is where a certain tyranny takes hold and perfection no longer declares an existing reality, but it becomes "perfectionism," the imposition of an impossible standard, commanding a reality to be what is not now. We fail to recognize perfection as emerging, a future possibility, and instead it undermines our present reality. *Psychology Today* (November 18, 2016)[2] offered nine indications which

---

[2] https://www.psychologytoday.com/us/blog/better-perfect/201611/9-signs-you-might-be-perfectionist (8/15/2019)

suggest you might be a perfectionist. They are: *1) You think in all-or-nothing terms; 2) You think, and then act, in extremes; 3) You can't trust others to do a task correctly, so you rarely delegate; 4) You have demanding standards for yourself and others; 5) You have trouble completing a project because you think there is always something more you can do to make it better; 6) You use the word "should" a lot; 7) Your self-confidence depends on what you accomplish and how others react to you; 8) You tend to fixate on something you messed up; and 9) You procrastinate, or avoid situations where you think you might not excel.* I offer these as a practical look at what the tyranny of perfection can lead us to, an absolute extreme view of life imposed on others and our self, that undermines one's sense of self. We end up fixating on our failures and at the same time denying them. In doing so we limit our sense of future possibilities. The tyranny is a trap of endless self-criticism and no true sense of personal satisfaction, no real happiness. So before we give in to this tyranny we need to appreciate several important realities.

The first two chapters of this work are the most critical and perhaps may be a challenge to some, so a little more of an introduction to these two chapters here will be helpful. First off, in chapter one, we face the myth of perfection, the false belief that the perfect, at least as it is commonly understood, is the point of life. This may be difficult because it seems that in the Christian Scriptures perfect is often used, so we may think that we must be perfect. Matthew most clearly exhorts us to a kind of perfection. He tells us "Be perfect, therefore, as your heavenly Father is perfect" (5:48). And we see the young man who fulfilled all the commands of the law, but still desired to do more: "Jesus said to him, 'If you wish to be perfect, go, sell your possessions, and give the money to the poor, and you will have treasure in heaven; then come, follow me'" (19:21). St. Paul in Romans 12:2 writes "Do not be conformed to this world, but be transformed by the renewing of your minds, so that you may discern what is the will of God— what is good and acceptable and perfect." However, in these texts, perfection (τελείοις) is understood more as a coming to fullness, a maturity, or completion. It has a sense of the future-possible that is coming to be in the present, an ordering of life here and now toward a time of fulfilment. Where the tyranny of perfection steps in, is with its failure to see the present reality, the now-moment, and dictates that the future-perfect must be the now-real. The college student who thinks he or she is inadequate because their grade point isn't a 4.0; or the teen who hates himself or herself because they don't match the photo-shopped images in the media; or the 30-something person who is miserable because they are trying to keep up with the Joneses; or the pensioner who feels useless and no longer of value, they are all victims of the tyranny of perfection. Living like this becomes oppressive. We fail to embrace our present given reality, to live in the now, but instead falsely try to live as if, in a make believe reality. Don't get me wrong, there are people living in the now who do embody a sense of perfection that is not tyrannical, who realize that they have been given a grace, and who use it well for the greater good. They embody a sense of genuineness and integrity that comes from a humble heart and what we see as perfection in them, they simply see as life, as their being genuine. It is our failure to trust the "now," that unique moment where we engage life, wherein the kind of doubt and mistrust, a false sense of perfection, is able to feed on and shred away at our self-confidence, our genuine self-awareness.

Chapter two is a look at the role of suspicion in creating this climate of mistrust. In this first book of the trilogy, we see the impact of Sigmund Freud (1856-1939) whose psycho-analytical approach has cast suspicion on our most basic human pleasure and we are never good enough. It may not be readily apparent, but Freud's approach has wrongly shackled true pleasure with a false notion of perfection. Freudian suspicion focuses on the wrongness of life, our fear of loss and our envy. Sadly, this is what makes us unhappy, unable to delight in the realities of life now. Compare Freud's psychosexual analysis, in which an infant's first development is focused on pleasure with that of Erik Erikson (1902-1994) and his psychosocial analysis which sees the first development stage as being about trust. Even Freud's stages (oral, anal, phallic, latent, and genital) alienate one from the most fundamental embodiment of existence, human sexual pleasure. It is this suspicion of human pleasure that leaves us feeling alienated, alone, and incomplete. Imagine life as a page of dots and you are too afraid to connect the dots. You will never see what picture emerges. Freudian self-alienation has contributed much to the tyrannical sense of perfection by focusing so much on what is wrong that we have compartmentalized life itself.

True perfection is about our becoming, an unfolding in the now, that is, one's fulfillment in life. In order to see this, we are aided by what the Ancients called the "transcendals" of Truth, Beauty and Goodness. Together these three form a "Mystical Braid" that requires their interplay and unity.

Chapters three through five show us how these three fundamental values of Truth, Beauty, and Goodness, enable us to live in the "becoming now" and help us to overcome the alienated life. We can see the inter-connectedness of science, art, and religion. For far too long they have been seen as oppositional, as incompatible and distinct. We have distorted the delightful pleasure these bring to an integrated way of life. In these three chapters we engage the correctives to the tyrannical hold that perfectionism has in people's lives. Rather than falling prey to the division and compartmentalization of life, these three transcendentals offer us a relational way of living.

Finally, in chapter six we are able to appreciate what true perfection means as the "just rightness" of life. That is to say that it is in the virtuous life where happiness is found and the human can flourish. While in chapter seven we find that it is the theological virtue of love which undoes the tyrannical chains of false perfection and our mistrust of life. Love as a paramount virtue affords us a way to discover the perfection of imperfection. The conclusion, chapter eight, looks at our taming the tyrant of perfection in our life and the Mystical Braid's helping us to find Truth, and Beauty, and Goodness once again. "In God We Trust" remains a hollow slogan if we don't first learn to trust one another, that delightfully imperfect perfection of being human.

Chapter One
The Myth of Perfection

Years ago when I was a college student I read a poem by the American writer, X. J. Kennedy entitled "Nothing in Heaven Functions as it Ought." The title really says it all. The first stanza catalogues a squeaky gate, Peter's broken spectacles, and angels, coughing in the choir. While the first line of the second stanza has haunted me, it declares: "But Hell, sleek Hell, hath no freewheeling part." This has always made me think that perhaps for perfectionists, heaven would be their Hell. We tend to think of perfection as being flawless, or being finished, something of the highest excellence. But in life that is difficult to really achieve, we are always a work in progress. I have found in my experience that the perfect is terribly overrated. In fact, I have found comfort in the imperfection of perfection itself. People who think they need to be perfect are pretty boring. They are limited by a standard that restricts the range within which they must function, they live restricted lives. The tyranny of perfection is this, it cannot abide the brokenness of life, human frailty and sin. Perfectionism is a kind of avarice for more, a failure to take delight in one's own being. But we mustn't assume that it is about things. Rather it is about our relation to things, our attitude and co-dependency on things that is the issue.

I recall working with someone in spiritual direction who shared a saying taught to him as a child but still fresh in his imagination: "Good, better, best. Never let it rest. Until the good is better, and the better best." This saying, attributed to St. Jerome, seems ambitious if not impossible. I could sense the impossible burden and high expectation under which this man labored as a child and now as an adult. Goodness is the goal, not perfection. An important lesson in life, I have found, is summed up in the saying, "Don't let the perfect become the enemy of the good." Various scholars and philosophers have echoed this in one form or another through the centuries, but even so, it is a hard lesson to learn. Shakespeare, in *King Lear* wrote "Striving to better, oft we mar what is well." Satisfaction is the ability to see what is enough, to take the really real as sufficient. In our consumerist world Mick Jagger of the Stones lamented "I can't get no satisfaction." The notions of "more" and "too much" mark a fine line between satisfaction and disappointment, a lesson I learned in the art of blowing bubbles or balloons. "More" always seems a good goal to achieve but "too much" can destroy it all and you are left with nothing except gum on your face or fragments of your burst balloon cast all around you.

So how do we get trapped into this myth of perfection? Why do we think that more is better? I think it has to do with our inability to know what is enough, our ability to accept the limits of life itself. Unlike Goldilocks we fail to learn the lesson of things being "just right". Rather, the myth of perfection is about more, having more, being more, getting more. Things are never "just right" and life as it is, is disappointing. In my memory there is a marvelous line in one of the movie versions of Charles Dickens' "A Christmas Carol" when Mrs. Cratchit says, "Strange thing 'enough', to those who have too much there is never enough, but for those who have too little, there is always just enough." Although I haven't found the actual source for this quotation, it has remained in my memory and it is very true. The myth of perfection is fundamentally about emotional and psychological greed, not knowing what is enough. The sad issue is our failure to learn what it means to be satisfied. We set ourselves up for unhappiness if we fail to learn the lesson of "enough-ness." We become gluttons, workaholics, or perfectionists because we do not know balance or harmony in life. One of the truly amazing sights for a child is seeing an object balanced on the end of stick, or a teeter-totter when both people balance each other. One of the remarkable realities, when we are older, is the balance among people in society called justice. Sadly, instead of happiness and satisfaction we have become obsessed with the avarice of more, more and more. A perfect score, a perfect spouse, a perfect child, a perfect home, a perfect job, all become oppressive if they are not being measured in terms of happiness and real moral virtue in life.

This then is the modern myth of perfection's tyranny — "You are not good enough!" and along with that, "You can only be happy if you be/do/have more!" This is the real sin of over-indulgence and greed. But why does it seem that we are so trapped in this addiction of more? I think one of the issues is that we have wandered away from the real worth and value of reality, alienating ourselves from the world as it really is. You see, the fact of the matter is that reality is a remarkably marred existence with chinks, cracks, tears, and flaws. Certainly things grow and increase, but things also die and decline. To the degree that we deny reality, or fail to truly know reality, to that degree we become enslaved by the illusion of a false sense of our self and of our world. The world becomes a grey and joyless place.

Stop and think about it for a moment. For us, as being fully human, reality is always about the present, the here and now, the becoming-now. By the gift of our mind and our imagination we explore ways to make reality accessible beyond the time and space limits, but the reality is as it is. A past reality has an historical existence and a future reality has a potential or possible existence, but the given-ness of reality grounds us in the here and now. In the classic poem "Ulysses," Alfred Lord Tennyson captures the mind of a legendary Greek hero as he recalled his life and his aged self. As the poem nears its end, Ulysses is aware that his life had been lived and now before him lies a new reality. These words I have found powerful ever since I first read them: "…Tho' much is taken, much abides; and tho' / We are not now that strength which in old days / Moved earth and heaven, that which we are, we are;…"[3] Why is this given-ness, this "that which we are," important? Only by taking life in the here and now, this place, this time, can we see the intricate relationship of good and evil, of what is and of what might or may be. The myth of perfection rips one from this given-ness, the ground of one's being, and

---

[3] https://www.poetryfoundation.org/poems/45392/ulysses. [3/5/2019] Poetry Foundation © 2019

offers a mirage in its place. For example, the Greek philosopher Plato in about 380 B.C. wrote *The Republic*, a classic work treating a hypothetical city-state ruled by a philosopher king. Sir Thomas More in 1516 A.D. described a fictional island called "Utopia" in a work by the same name [A bit of irony is that the word "utopia" literally means "no place"]. H. G. Wells wrote his "A Modern Utopia" in 1905 depicting a single global order ruled by a voluntary samurai society. In all of these works the authors criticize the failings of the society in which they lived. The realities of their world prompted them to see in a possible perfect, the given-ness in their present "now," hopefully to be transformed by moral choices yet to be made. The important distinction between fact, the given-ness of life, and fantasy, the pretend or imagined life, is critical for genuine human flourishing. In this life, there will always be a tension between what is and what might be. This confronts us with the moral choice to develop, or to decay, to live, or to die, to dwell in the past, or to daydream about the future, but reality exists only in the now. This is the tyranny -- a perfectionist thinks happiness is out there somewhere and fails to notice it, already right here.

How does the tyranny of perfection get it wrong? After all isn't perfect, by definition the best? Allow me to offer an example. The European Union in 1994 legislated the standards of green bananas in a law called by the media the "bendy banana law." It legislated the perfect size and shape for bananas. The law was replaced in 2011, but it demonstrates how standards of the so-called perfect are impractical. The myth of perfection fails to realize that growth and change constitute a living process of becoming from potentiality to actuality. Thomas Aquinas, who lived in the 13th century, unsettled the *status quo* at the University of Paris by shifting the focus away from potentiality, the realm of the ideal, to actuality, the thing in itself, reality. This distinction allowed him to address the world as it is and not as a shadowy manifestation of the ideal. For Aquinas, who followed much of the thought of Aristotle, the relationship between what he called matter, the stuff of a thing, and its form, the organizing principle of matter, did not exist separate from one another. For him you couldn't separate the material element, seeing it as the evil or imperfect bit, from the whole, it is a substantial reality [*hylemorphism*], a whole as it is, in a sense "the good the bad, and the ugly" as it is. For example, a slab of clay can be shaped into a variety of items from plates, to cups, to ashtrays but these items only exist once the artisan has bestowed each their proper form and the clay retains its existence. In this way of thinking, reality is about a thing's actuality and individuality, it is about integrity and uniqueness. It is how we know and define our world, as well as appreciate both otherness and uniqueness. Here is where we can see the myth of perfection undermining both integrity and uniqueness by its denying the really real of a thing, or sadly of a person. Such denial plants the gnawing cancer of self-doubt and self-alienation – *there is something wrong with me and/or there must be something wrong with you*. The sage wisdom of the oracle of Delphi to "know thyself" is critical, but for us, we need to know the self, the true self, which is only borne of true knowledge. Such knowledge, as Ulysses says, "is, that which is."

I would like to tell you the story of two sculptors who were both given a flawless block of Carrera marble in order to carve a memorial for a very wealthy patron. Each artisan worked long days and nights chiseling away creating their masterpiece. As the one worked, the other person was plagued by fear and self-doubt that his work would be inferior. So he chiseled and rubbed away day and night trying to make the marble slab obey his demands for an ideal image that, in his mind, was to be so perfect. For months both men labored away but the fearful artisan seemed never satisfied with what that day's efforts brought. He lamented that the stone was inferior (though in fact both slabs were practically identical), he complained that the light was too poor (though each had the same light with which to work), and that his assistants were dolts (though they were very capable artisans). With each feature of his sculpture that appeared, he felt it was flawed, so he cut and scraped more and more which only made him look with disdain on the impact it had on the other features. The more he tried to fix the sculpture the more he chiseled and rasped and filed away until his block of flawless Carrera marble was nothing but rubble. Out of despair he became despondent and thought to take his life.

Meanwhile the other sculptor began each day with a simple prayer, "Dear Lord, show me Thy face. Allow me to discover you, hidden in my day." Each day he did what he could and accepted what he had done, realizing that there was more yet to discover, hidden in the stone. Each day his prayer remained the same and each night he went to bed trusting that the next day he would discover more. As time went on, and he discovered more and more of what had been hidden, he soon realized the "Face of Christ" seeming to stare back at him from the stone. Finally, the man took a good look at the sculpting and said to himself: "Alas nothing lies hidden and I have completed my task." Just then the marble face seemed to speak to the artist and said: "Well done, for you chose not to define but to discover, not to impose but to dispose." The "Face of Christ" set in marble was bruised, anguished, cut and pierced by thorns. Not at all what we might call "pretty" but it was real, true, and genuine. When the wealthy patron saw the end result of each sculptor's efforts he said: "One poor soul reduced to rubble the gift that had been given to him, while the other found his soul hidden in the stone, simply by removing the bits that were false, untrue." A few months later the first artist saw the "Face of Christ" made by his rival and realized he was seeing himself for the first time. The face knew his pain and struggle and it moved him to tears. From then on he embraced his flaws and found true joy.

The myth of perfection enslaves us in self-doubt, in a fixation on mistakes, confined by impossibly high standards. This is why we need to acknowledge it as undermining genuine human flourishing. In one sense, what this myth of perfection tells us is that we have no need of salvation since we are capable of reaching perfection on our own, but in the end it proves to be self-defeating. What becomes our chief concern is avoiding, rather than being. We fixate on avoiding failure to the point that we cannot tolerate our need for conversion, the honest and mature acceptance of our flaws and failures. It can even make us, in the end, so idealistic that the world itself cannot be accepted and we must fix it, somehow, it doesn't really matter how, but we are bound to fix it. It is much easier to tell ourselves the fault lies out there than to admit that we all have faults. It is only in admitting our flaws that we come to discover hidden in them something truly remarkable, for they hold the kernel of something that needs to grow.

The Canadian singer and songwriter Leonard Cohen's 1992 Columbia Records Album, *The Future,* has a song called "The Anthem" and its refrains holds a powerful lesson about flaws and brokenness in life. Cohen sings in his raspy voice: *Ring the bells that still can ring / Forget your perfect offering / There is a crack, a crack in everything / That's how the light gets in.* You see, the myth of perfection only has power if and when we deny the possibility of the imperfect, the frail and the flawed reality that is human life. Light enters through the cracks in our world, in the mistakes, the flaws, yes even in the mystery of sin. One of the great twists of life is found in the Christian Easter Vigil at the *Exultet* when the sin of Adam and Eve is transformed in the light of Christ as they sing the words "O happy fault that earned for us so great, so glorious a Redeemer!" (*O felix culpa, quæ talem ac tantum méruit habére Redemptórem!*). Here is the classic crack that let in the light of salvation. But why have we allowed this tyranny of perfection to enslave us, to trap us in a false notion of the perfect as being better than the good?

In the next few chapters we will look at the doubt and mistrust that have made us deny, or treat as suspect, things like truth, and beauty, and goodness, or science, art, and religion. Plato called these "transcendentals," really we might think of them as ultimate values, for they empower human imagination. Finally, we will then see how the tyranny of perfection offers a false destiny, ignoring the brokenness of life, and ultimately the lesson of love. The tyranny of perfection robs us of the light that enters in through the cracks and flaws, that are hidden in the mess of life.

Chapter Two

Doubt and Mistrust

I imagine we all know the famous parable from India about a group of blind people who came across an elephant. Each person felt a different part of the creature and explained what it was based on their experience. One person, who felt the trunk, said it was a large snake. The other, who touched the ear, said it was a great fan. Another who took its tail, said it was a rope, and so the story goes. Each person believed the other was lying and harsh words turned to violent blows. In the midst of their fighting a sighted person came and asked them the meaning of their quarrel. After listening to each person, the sighted person described the creature as a whole, and the blind individuals realized that each was only partly right. This parable illustrates how we come to judge things based on our limited subjective experience. How we often times interpret the whole of a thing based only on a part. It also illustrates an interesting philosophical question and that is the nature of interpretation, or *hermeneutics* -- the meaning of written, verbal and non-verbal communication.

It was believed that the ancient Greek god Hermes delivered the divine messages and was considered the one who bestowed language and speech, but he also could be a liar and a trickster. Language, meanings, and interpretations can be both truths and/or lies. So you see, the divine oracles rested on learning and knowing the right meaning. Aristotle's work "On Interpretation" (*Peri Hermeneias*) philosophically explored language and logic. Our ideas and the words we use to express our ideas are not always received in the way or manner we intend. Even some words play tricks on our understanding. So, for example, if I say "the bark was harsh" do I mean a tree trunk's bark, or a dog's bark, or the crusty coating on my pork roast? Words and meanings are open to interpretation but especially religious, classical and political texts. Because they are shared, they require interpretation and demand some sense of integrity. For example, it is wrong and a false interpretation to claim that references to the "Gay '90s" is due to homosexual culture simply because the word "gay" can mean such today. No the context of the 1890s and its freedom and carefreeness are the context for understanding that time as the "Gay '90s." Interpreting meanings of the Bible, or the U.S. Constitution, or Shakespeare's writings, require a contextual appreciation, a dynamic relation between the author's intention, the text's implication and the reader's or listener's understanding. For example, in a heated conversation the phrase "With all due respect" might sound like an honorable recognition of your opponent but in fact, in some contexts, it can be a sarcastic coded way of saying "if your position warranted respect I would give it, but it does not, so I don't." Politicians and lawyers can be masterful at doublespeak, when their words seem to say one thing, but they mean another. This is also known as equivocation, using words that suggest a meaning other than what is commonly understood. The most infamous example was in the 1990's when a politician said "I did not have sexual relations with that woman" and claimed not to have lied, given the legal definition of the phrase "sexual relations." So we see that what a person says, and what their words mean, are open to interpretation. The legal industry makes a grotesque fortune from parsing words and interpreting the law, so the point often is not the truth, but what people can be convinced into believing to be true, is truer than the true.

As I mentioned earlier, the French philosopher Jean Paul Ricoeur (1913-2005) sought to understand human interpretation or hermeneutics and coined the phrase "school of suspicion" for one interpretive approach he detected. In so doing he addressed a tendency to highlight or unmask the less likely or sinister meanings of a text. Ricoeur also saw another, more common way of interpretation as aimed at being faithful to the text and wanting to restore its authentic meaning. However, it was this suspicious approach that created doubt and mistrust, false assumptions and false narratives we find today. While this approach sought to expose the suspected meanings, it made common discourse difficult. Ricoeur identified three popular theorists of the 19th century as the "Masters of Suspicion" and they were: Sigmund Freud, Karl Marx, and Friedrich Nietzsche. Each has significantly sown mistrust. Pleasure, wealth and power, in moderation can serve a noble and virtuous purpose. However, the problem arises when abuse of pleasure, wealth and power corrupt and distort the human project. The problem with these "Masters of Suspicion" is that they have distorted our way of thinking so that vice rather than virtue is the starting point. Pleasure, wealth, and power are the masked culprits hiding behind every text, every statement, every thought. As noted in the Preface, it is these three thinkers who have shaped our cultural mistrust. Chances are that even now, as you the reader reflect on this, you may be thinking "eat, drink and be merry" or "money is the root of all evil" or "power corrupts" and rightly suspect pleasure, wealth, and power. So the fine line is really about virtue, but if you deny the virtuous person exists, then these three – pleasure, wealth, and power -- are always the suspected motives in life. Consequently, this trilogy will explore how we restore virtue so that we may employ pleasure, wealth and power wisely and rightly.

In this work I am particularly interested in the impact that Sigmund Freud (1856-1939) has had in our appreciation and understanding of perfection. [In the other works of this trilogy I will examine the impacts of Marx and Nietzsche.] In a sense, I wish to unmask some of the hidden realities of Freudian psycho-analysis and its role in our misguided notion of human perfection, which leaves us suspicious of all pleasure. For Freud, the young field of psychology afforded him a novel way to understand human behavior. The nineteenth and early twentieth centuries were very prudish, very "Victorian" and very taboo, sexually speaking. His efforts to understand consciousness and its hidden and repressed awareness of sexuality, ties into issues of perfection and psycho-sexual analytics. His famous "Oedipus complex" planted the seed of an impossible standard and fear of failure compounded by feelings of inadequacy. For Freud this is seen in his notion that boys suffer from "castration anxiety" and girls from "penis envy." This profound concern of loss and absence in Freud, I believe, contributed to the oppressive dynamic of false perfection. Fear of loss (castration) and absence (envy) undermine one's capacity for wholesome integration, and a failure to find delight in the imperfect.

For Freud it is the sexual drive paradigm and mix of pleasure and guilt that creates an almost impossible expectation in children and in adolescence. There seems to be a fixation in Freud on repressed sexual scenarios from a person's childhood. Simply put, in his 1920 essay "Beyond the Pleasure Principle" and his 1923 work *The Ego and the Id,* he puts forth a model of the human psyche as an unconscious and impulsive part; driven by the principle of pleasure, called the "id" and another part that is critical and moralizing, called the "super-ego;" with a third part, called the "ego" that brokers between the desires and drives of the other two. One can see the influence of Hegel's dialectical model that dominated 20th century thinking.[4] The notion of thesis, anti-thesis, synthesis requires a conflict or struggle between two alternatives achieving resolution in a third. Marx will use this in his theory of class struggle. However, in the human psyche it creates a binary framing of success vs. failure, healthy vs unhealthy, normal vs abnormal. In 2005 Richard Layard rightly observed, "In the last thirty years practical psychology has been through a revolution. Before that, it was focused heavily on what had gone

---

[4] See Clark Butler's essay "Hegel and Freud: A Comparison" in *Philosophy and Phenomenological Research* Vol. 36, No. 4 (Jun., 1976), pp. 506-522

wrong with people. The dominant idea, from Freud, was that people are victims of their childhood experiences and can only become all right if they can relive and understand their past."[5]

In Freud I see a fundamental problem that casts pleasure and particularly human sexual pleasure as the wild part of the psyche, or the id, which must be controlled, regulated and restricted. In other places, Freud sees a conflict between the life drive (*Eros*) and the death drive (*Thanatos*). So in one sense, not only has Freud imposed on us a binary mindset of mistrusting our ability to find pleasure and take delight in pleasure, but in the end, we even repress the playful and silly parts of life, as G. K. Chesterton observed "It is easy to be solemn, it is so hard to be frivolous." Pleasure, especially sexual pleasures, are so mistrusted that it is taboo and reduced to being either repressed or exploited, which is tragic. We see this in society's struggle to understand (or failure to understand) a person's sexual orientation or gender as their unique given-ness—the truth of a person from which one's life truth is lived. It is the false hope of perfection that refuses to see in the challenging and genuine reality of "that which it is" but instead pretends, redefines or re-assigns reality. Sigmund Freud has played a singularly major role in self-doubt and our failure to trust, by inventing a division within the human psyche or what we may also call the soul (*anima* in Latin, *psyche* in Greek). He fails to appreciate this

---

[5] Richard Layard, *Happiness: Lessons from a New Science* (New York: Penguin Press, 2005) p. 195.

Chapter Two – Doubt and Mistrust

fundamental truth, that we were made for happiness and that happiness is borne of our knowing and loving. Both knowing and loving require not only a subject, the knower or lover, but an object as well, the known or loved. The most satisfying object for us is another person or ultimately, God. Once we are able to accept the given-ness of life, the seemingly flawed and imperfect mix of human life, do we find that it is rich in discovery and desire, rich in knowing and loving, and then do we find an innocence restored.

Modernity has tricked us into chasing after perfection and it is done at the expense of reality. It is the ancient evil that tempts us to be other than who we truly are. It was the devil's primal lie in Eden who said, "No, you shall not die; for God knows that when you eat of it, your eyes will be opened and you will be like God knowing good and evil" (Genesis 3:4-5). Doubt and mistrust remain the most diabolic of devices, for they literally divide, alienate, and throw us apart. [Diabolic comes from the Greek $\delta\iota\alpha$ - which means apart, and $\beta\alpha\lambda\lambda\epsilon\iota\nu$ - which means to throw or cast.] Think about it, we are living in one of the most divisive and contentious of times. All of our high-minded ideals and sophisticated technology have done little to unite us. In fact, they have been co-opted into the web of doubt and mistrust. Journalism, academia, social media, all perpetuate the doubt and mistrust spawned from the fear we have to simply be -- the given limits of our humanity. Instead, we chase after a false perfection, a global Utopia that destroys difference by its conformity and amalgamates the aggregates under the veneer of a false façade.

Doubt and mistrust seem to be the by-products of our expectation that all must be perfect. True perfection is not about a future state of being, but it is about becoming-now. Let me say that again: True perfection is not about a future state of being but it is about becoming-now. The Latin root *perficere* means "to finish or to bring to completion," so in this life true perfection must always be about a becoming, and the tyranny of perfection is our expectation that it be done, finished, completed. Now as far as inanimate objects are concerned, certain standards and norms can be set and the thing can be judged against these standards, but for animate beings, for things with life, there is always a becoming. In this life perfection would come only in death, the *consummatum est* of life, the last uttered words uttered by Christ.

In the midst of this life of becoming we know our flaws and failures but we also discover promise and potentials. Becoming is not without purpose, but it is a purpose that unfolds in the fullness of time (*kairos*), and is not measured with an expiration date. Three things in particular guide our becoming, for they order us to that ultimate reality. In the next three chapters we will explore how each of these properties of human existence move us beyond stagnation and decay to fullness. The ancient thinkers (Socrates, Plato and Aristotle) understood them as transcendentals, they are: Truth, Beauty, and Goodness. They teach us and engage us in the art of becoming through the fields of science, art, and religion. Each helps us to face the tyranny of perfection and together they show us what ultimate perfection is meant to be and become. We need to appreciate more fully the interplay of science, art, and religion in order to tame the tyrant of perfection. They are part of a Mystical Braid of life.

Chapter Two – Doubt and Mistrust

Chapter Three

"You Can't Handle the Truth!"

Years ago in American courtrooms a witness swore an oath to "tell the truth, the whole truth, and nothing but the truth," invoking the absolute divine saying, "so help me God." But truth in the 21st century has become obscured, even denied its universal validity. Instead people talk about individual or personal truths – "Oh that may be true for you but it is not true for me." So, like Pontius Pilate we ask, what do we mean by the concept Truth?

Every small child seems to have a difficult association with truth, especially when a parent demands them to tell the truth. Fear can alter our sense of truth, reward and punishment certainly play in a child's sense of what the truth looks like. The immature person never really does befriend truth, which only comes with experience and understanding. In our post-Enlightenment, scientific world truth has become something of an absolute verifiability which makes it rather rare. The truth is that Truth is more elusive. That is why I like the insights of Martin Heidegger (1889-1976) who made a distinction between truth (*veritas*) as an undeniably verifiable reality and truth (*alētheia*) as an elusively disclosive reality, evanescent like a puff of smoke. But why is this important? Why did he bother? A major reason is that we as human beings are wired in such a way that we desire or want to engage the true, to freeze-frame it and nail it down, thereby distorting it. In the movie

A Few Good Men a military lawyer named Lt. Daniel Kaffee played by Tom Cruise interrogates a very hardened senior officer named Colonel Nathan R. Jessep, played by Jack Nicholson. In the dramatic and heated exchange, the lawyer declares "I want the truth!" and the intense response shouted back by the colonel is "You can't handle the truth!" This may be more true than we want to admit.

Desiring the Truth and accepting the Truth are two dimensions of a profound reality that we would rather ignore or deny, and that is integrity. We often distort or bend the truth in order to fabricate a version of things that we think should or could be. But if a thing is true it is true because it is, what it is, as it is. This is an aspect of existence -- *it is*. Heidegger's notion of disclosive or revealing truth is closer to what is true, truer than what we think or say is true in our minds or defined by our concepts. Language strains to name our ideas and concepts which are groping to connect with the reality. For example, if you describe something as being blue, is that really adequate? So why is this important? It is important because given our basic drive for the true, the genuinely real, it allows for the dynamic of life, of human life, and this is change, growth, becoming. Truth is evanescent and enduring, concealing and revealing, there isn't just one blue.

John Cardinal Newman (1801-1890) remarked that "To live is to change. To live well is to change often." So life, by its very nature is a changing thing, and so, truth for us, rather than a frozen, stagnant reality, is a dynamic thing. The challenge lies in our capacity to grasp complex reality;

it requires a dynamic that must have an infinite capacity. Life, is never about the things known, but it is about the art of knowing! How is it that we know things or people? Both of these demand their unique mode of knowing. So often people say you can't argue with facts. But that is nonsense, facts are exactly what every argument is about. Why is that? I make a distinction between facts and data. Both are essential to the art or science of knowing but they are quite different, and the terms say it all. "Data" is the plural for *datum* which in Latin means something given. Data then presents itself and we make something of what is given. A "fact" or *factum* in Latin means a thing done from the Latin *facere*, "to do". So you see, the fact is that you can't argue with data, what is given, but once we try to name it, know it, conceptualize it, we fashion the data into facts. All facts come already smudged by a layer that distorts the reality, but we foolishly think that facts are our infallible handle on reality. Facts need to be argued because Truth is elusive and disclosive, revealing and concealing of its nature. Our biggest mistake is to try and domesticate Truth rather than enjoying the task and challenge of learning to live with it. This is more what science is meant to be. It is discovering and engaging reality, NOT exploiting and commercializing it. For the classics "the True" was one of the transcendent realities or one of the highest values, along with "Beauty" and "Goodness." Together these three are what connect us to existence and they provide a means for the human project to touch reality through a Mystical Braid of logic, aesthetics and ethics. These are three critical aspects of human flourishing and we engage them actively, dynamically in science, art, and religion. I will say more about art and religion, beauty and goodness, in the following chapters but for now I want to focus on the True and our Logic of Life, our need for *scientia* (science).

"Science" since the Enlightenment has held a place of honor in our modern world. It's emphasis on the empirical, mathematical, and verifiable, its method of purpose-procedure-results, engages, and at times, has sought to master the world. Often we hear the phrase "Science and Technology" implying a mastery. Technology may be defined as "the application of scientific knowledge for practical purposes, especially in industry" as does The Oxford Dictionary.[6] But this is only one aspect and a reduction of what science is meant to be. It reduces science to the pragmatic and productive which reduces Truth to an equational formula. Imagine if the association were "Science and Harmony" how different and fuller science becomes. As part of the Mystical Braid, Science is wedded to Truth and enables us to connect to or belong to existence itself. However, part of the tyranny of perfection is to wrongly expect science to be the definitive and incontestable perfect proof of things. Fortunately, Truth is not so trapped. To do this is to hold to a very limited notion of proof. The word "proof" comes from the Latin *probare*, which means "to test and find a thing good." A proof is more an approval on our part and we commonly tend to accept or approve the results. But there are different kinds of things we test and approve. One class of things would be

---

[6] https://en.oxforddictionaries.com/definition/technology 5/8/2019

inanimate material objects, like a rock, we examine the quality and quantity of such things. Here is where we render a judgment, and approve the qualitative difference a lump of coal has and that of a diamond. Or we quantitatively recognize the value of one ton of coal for heating in the winter and a diamond set in a ring given as a pledge of marriage. No one would seriously seek to prove that 2+2=4 is false. They might demonstrate that the decimal system we use to understand isn't the only possible system and that the equation would be meaningless in a binary or octal system.

This is important in our appreciating the limits of science and that is this, **it has limits**! Science can only suggest to us that a thing is, or is not, may or may not be, this and not that. We must interpret or probe how a thing is. For example, prove that 4=100! On face value we would dismiss such an equation as false and discredit anyone who believed such folly. However, it is a true equation once we realize that 4 in the decimal system equals 100 in the binary system. Science has limits and truth is far more pliable than we think. But we are talking about things, inanimate, material things. Science engages yet another dimension of human existence and that is the animate and immaterial reality, the physical and the meta-physical. We distinguish between the hard sciences and the soft sciences, or natural and social sciences, based on a believed difference in precision and rigor. However, when we deal with human existence science is a help, but it is fallible. No one has deciphered the formula for true love, no one has decoded the DNA of charity or justice. These are realities which require philosophical, theological and moral tools, tools which are part of wisdom's craft. Good science as part of the Mystical Braid employs proofs and demonstration to either clearly show that a thing is so or that it is plausible or that it might be. The limits of science can be seen in the intense debate in society as to the life of a fetus or the global warming of the planet. Science here can only suggest what may be True but Truth requires more.

Science is both Technology and Harmony, which opens to us the mystery of Truth and our connection with existence itself. In this interplay of Truth, Science opens to us a more richly textured universe. Here we encounter a different understanding of perfection and a reprieve from its tyranny. For it is in this fulsome sense of Science that we encounter the notion of degrees, the concept of more or less. We've all heard the saying "more is better." Well that's not right, because there is such a thing as too much, which distorts and burdens reality. It is the Goldilocks principle of "just right" that allows gradation to teach us about the end or purpose of things. Science that connects us to Truth bestows a special pleasure to life. So what does this teach us about the perfection of things? It shows us that we must balance life to attain the "just right" reality. Now "just right" says a lot! "Justice" is fundamentally about relationships that are ordered to the good and "rightness" is about choices ordered to the true. Thomas Aquinas in the *Summa Theologiae* (I q.2, a.3) asks if it is possible for there to be an absolute of every good and true, of every just and right, and for that to actually have existence. If so, Thomas holds that we would probably call that God, or some absolute reality. It is the perfection, the fulfilment of all possible goodness and truth, and more, it actually has existence. This way of thinking puts perfection in its "just right" frame, as not tyrannical, but in fact inspirational. We strive to become! This is the task of human existence – to be and to become "just right." How do we do this? How we understand this project is the most critical task of a person's life. It addresses how one is uniquely on a journey from being to becoming. This is why science, truth, and a logic of life are so essential in facing the tyranny of perfection.

As with any journey we look for signs to guide us on the way. The absolute ideal is that beacon which guides us on the calm waters and stormy seas of life. Truth as disclosive and elusive is one such guide post. Science and scientific understanding are certainly important, but there are more indicators of life that we need to examine. The Mystical Braid is the interplay of Truth, Beauty and Goodness as we see in Science, Art, and Religion, our logic, aesthetics and ethics. Sadly, today we have broken this inter-playfulness. The next two chapters will further develop how this Mystical Braid restores a more meaningful sense of perfection and perfect-ability.

Chapter Three – "You Can't Handle the Truth!"

Chapter IV

Mirror, Mirror on the Wall...

In the classic 1937 Disney animation of *Snow White and the Seven Dwarfs* the image of the evil queen asking her Magic Mirror as to who was the fairest in the land remains a vivid memory for many. The Magic Mirror always told the truth and one day the truth was not what the queen cared to hear. The answer to her question was: "My Queen you are the fairest here so true. But Snow White is a thousand times more beautiful than you." We all know the horrific plot that ensues but what I'd like to focus on is the Magic Mirror as the instrument used to obtain truth, ultimately a moment of self-critical awareness. Here we see an important dynamic to Beauty and that is its capacity for deeper and greater human self-awareness and genuine self-identity. The evil queen beheld her own image in the mirror but it is in the question of "Beauty" that the queen confronts the Truth. Truth, as we saw in the previous chapter, provides us with a guide to life, a delight in living. As one of the transcendent realities Beauty connects us to existence, the given-ness of our life, but it is aided by Truth and our ability to engage Beauty. Ultimately we seek to discover True Beauty, who is the fairest in the land.

Beauty that is true confronts us with either an affirmation of our self-awareness or an envy that negates or wants to destroy beauty and the beautiful. Beauty has the capacity to draw us out to an engaging awareness of the world and to find it delightful, "genuinely pleasing." There is a pleasure in beauty, a pure and absolute pleasure in our encounter with beauty. We want to linger in the beautiful, to capture it in cameras or on canvas, to be, exist in it, because it gives us delight. There is an ecstatic quality to Beauty that lifts one out of the mundane, the common, to an encounter with the awe of existence. Beauty awakens our passion and desire to and for the Good, which is the third transcendent of the Mystical Braid we will see in chapter 5.

How then does this Beauty connect us to existence? How does it help us end the tyranny of perfection? Beauty engages a part of how we process and know the world differently from the empirical and scientific modes of Truth. For Beauty engages the personal and subjective encounter with the perceived beautiful object. Now such objects may be found in nature, as they are found in another person, or in thoughts and ideas, but they are all objects of Beauty. We can try to understand aspects of the beautiful in its overall sense of proportion, harmony, symmetry, balance, sensuality, and composition. In so doing it brings a sense of completion or satisfaction and a desire or longing in us. Our first response to the beautiful object is not analytical but appreciative, or aesthetic, not bothered by analysis but bathed in appreciation. Beauty allows us to engage our world free from the limits of rational argument, cognitive knowing, and allows us to engage the world in appreciative awareness – the aesthetics of life.

Chapter Four – Mirror, Mirror on the Wall. . .

Unless you are programmed or trained to process experience in second level reflection, most of us will engage our experiences of Beauty pre-reflectively. It is only once we engage our experience do we move from a "gut awareness" to explaining and justifying the "why" we find it beautiful. It is at the pre-cognitive "gut-level" that we register our like or dislike and fashion our opinions for or against accordingly. But in that threshold before we try to name the reality there is first a level of pleasure, of a pure joy that is without definition. I recall one time in particular when I was standing alongside the groom in the front of the altar just before the bride was to enter. I had worked with this couple leading up to the moment and I could tell he was nervous. Once the last groomsman and bridesmaid had taken their places, as the main doors were closed, the music paused and a new melody began. Just at that moment the doors flew open to reveal a beautiful woman, dressed in white, step into the doorway. At that moment this young, strong man at my side began to weep. I asked him if he was okay. Words at first failed him but then he uttered: "She is so beautiful. I don't deserve her." Well as I fought to keep my composure I recall thinking how powerful his words were. "The humble intelligence of the heart" to use Blessed Jordan of Saxony's phrase, sought to name the beauty. In that moment the overwhelming pleasure of this beauty that was so much more than appearances, touched his heart, he was brought to the humble heart that knows we are never deserving, good enough, strong enough, perfect enough, to deserve such pure delight. True pleasure shatters the shackles of tyrannical perfection and pride. It exposes us to a deep awareness that is there before a word is spoken, our humble self that is pure receptivity.

A baby's smile, a sunset in the summer sky, a moonrise against the starlit winter night, a companion, a true friend, or a loving spouse with whom we have grown old, these are all moments of intense delight and true pleasure. They are born of a Beauty that connects us to the ultimate values of life. It undoes the Freudian mistrust of pleasure, that tendency to suspect what is genuinely given, and restores a true delight to life. Beauty has the power to reclaim human sexuality from the dark corners where it is so easily exploited. Beauty allows us, as we saw with Truth, to engage the mystery of human existence. Beyond our words, beyond any utterance, Beauty is the infallible delight and purest pleasure of being. Perfection, that is false perfection, fails to cherish the becoming-ness of life, fails to encounter in the countless imperfections, a mysterious whole that allows us to glimpse true Beauty. Often, it is imperfectly and incompletely perceived, but Beauty is about the whole, the totality of life.

So the important lesson for us to learn about the perfectibility of the imperfect is that the ultimate, transcendent value of Beauty connects us to the pleasure and delight of existence itself, of creation. It is that constant doubt or suspicion that creeps into our awareness and distorts the truly beautiful. While Freud has helped us articulate and analyze psychological theory, and yet analysis can never fully name, or do justice to the mystery of another human being. Once we dismiss true pleasure and wrongly see it as merely part of the psycho-sexual "pleasure principle" we rob human sexuality of its greatest Beauty and that is delight. Robbed in such a way we mistrust our genuine attractions born of beauty and instead awkwardly second guess ourselves. We deny and distort the ultimate awareness of Beauty found in the imperfect, flawed and broken bits of life, its naked vulnerability.

What do I mean? Sadly, the marketing industry has exploited our delight in beauty, the simple pleasure of beholding the beautiful. We have even reduced our notion of being beautiful to the hollow status of being "attractive." Every effort is made to manipulate our human delight in attraction, to market products so they sell, politicians so they get elected, and life itself for nothing but selfish pleasure. Hedonism, a life built only on pleasure, void of true Beauty, fails to connect us to existence, the wonder of being-ness, of existence itself. This connection to creation takes delight in the beauty of becoming which is true perfection (*perficere*), as coming to completion.

In 1843 Hans Christian Anderson (1805-1875) wrote a classic fairy tale of a homely ugly little duckling who was born in a barn, mocked, ridiculed, belittled, but all the time, day by day the chick was growing up, maturing until one day that ugly duckling became a beautiful swan. But this process took time as the tale tells us. The difficult and miserable reality of becoming can mean rejection, alienation and isolation. Our own inner fears make us run away to a place of solitude as did the duckling. Several times in the tale the duckling is confronted with rejection, among the wild ducks and geese who were hunted down, the taunting of an old woman's cat and hen, and the farmer's noisy children all drove the duckling away. At each of these moments we see the cruel realities the duckling faces but what is not apparent is the unfolding of existence, the slow but sure becoming that Beauty brings to completion. It is in the solitude of winter, sheltered in a cave by the lake, where the duckling is transformed, the becoming of being that is the deepest pleasure. For you see, there is beauty in our coming to fullness, to what we are meant to be and become, that is a process, a maturing, a becoming. All throughout this tale of tyranny, perfection places a heavy burden on us to be something we are not, a denial of the existence that is ours with all its challenges and all its possibilities.

Beauty unfolds in our life; it takes time for us to see the connection to existence itself. The duckling couldn't see its potential coming to be from within, hidden from our eyes, the mystery of life beautifully unfolds. Rather than allowing the tyranny of perfection to dominate and destroy us we, like the duckling, winter in our woes, sheltering ourselves in those hollow places of life, our caves of solitude where, like a womb, life unfolds, life becomes. In our fairy tale the Beauty, the true perfection, is discovered not manufactured. Nowhere in the tale does the duckling resort to cosmetics, to surgery, to genetic engineering, but rather, she endures to undergo life, to suffer existence without giving up. For this is the real beauty of true perfection. It is the delightful pleasure of discovering who we truly are, to exist which means "to stand out," to emerge, to appear. For you see perfection is about becoming. One day the duckling faced her fears and left the cave no longer afraid to face reality and instead chose to enter into life. It was only at that moment when she saw herself reflected in the waters of the lake did she realize who she was. She didn't need a magical mirror but nature and creation itself reflected back her reality. That is the birth of Beauty, what true perfection is all about, the self-realization of "who I am." But there is more. The water's reflection was only one part of the discovery, it was now when the self-realization of her belonging is known, her properly relating to life. With that, the duckling took flight, not out of fear as before, but amid the beauty of the flock in flight, transcending, rising beyond life's limits.

Realization and relationship are the true key lessons of beauty that French writer Marie-Henri Beyle (1783-1842), also known as Stendhal, knew. He defined beauty simply as this: "the promise of happiness." The evil queen, as we saw from the start of this chapter, sought a vain beauty disconnected from existence itself, lacking self-realization and genuine relationships with others. How different the tale of true realization and relationship is found in the ugly duckling. For beneath the surface of things, deep within the being of that bird, was the hopeful promise of happiness coming to be. What we must learn is that perfection without a sense of beauty is a vain and hollow life. Such perfection is oppressive. But perfection that beholds the beautiful in life, that discovery born of self-realization and relationship, is the real pleasure of perfection, our becoming who we are meant to be. It is the aesthetics of life.

Chapter Four – Mirror, Mirror on the Wall. . .

Chapter V

"For Goodness Sake…"

Every Christmas we remind the children and we ourselves are reminded of being good. But the phrase "For Goodness Sake" has a couple of meanings depending on use. "For goodness sake, I can't believe it!" Or, "Oh for goodness sake are you still on the phone?" Both of these illustrate the alternatives as both surprise or annoyance. In this chapter we will see how the ultimate value of "the Good" serves to correct a false notion of perfection and more importantly restores trust in the foundational reality of existence. Perhaps now it is becoming clearer that the Mystical Braid of Truth, Beauty, and Goodness, these three ultimate values, serve as correctives to the tyranny of perfection by connecting us to the underlying reality of existence. Perhaps we should say the "out-standing" reality of existence, for that is what the word "existence" means. Truth, Beauty and Goodness overcome our mistrust of the world and allow us to "step out" – to exist! That simple act allows us to enjoy the act of living, to find genuine pleasure. Whereas Truth engages our understanding and Beauty the promise of happiness, it is Goodness that summons our desires, our longings and aspirations. There is a hunger in the human heart for the Good, an infinite capacity to enjoy the Good, but even so, a good is good not because we want it, but because it draws us into existence, our genuinely being and becoming.

I am reminded of a story of four friends vacationing together. They were going to swim in their host's pool. One person was at the pool before the others, but at first she felt the water to be too cold, so she gradually eased herself into the water. Slowly, in time she felt right at home, swimming and enjoying the water. Now another friend came out to join her and asked how it was. Knowing that her friend would probably not get in if she was told it was cold at first, the person in the water said "It's great, just jump right in." To her surprise the friend did, only to surface with that look of exhilaration and wonderment as her body too, almost instantaneously acclimated to the water. Yet another friend came out with no intention of even getting near the water. She sat at a distance, beyond the splash zone, to engage in friendly banter. The fourth friend never left the house, never even wanted to join them. This episode illustrates for me the reality of Goodness and its role in the moral life, that is our living-well, living for the sake of goodness. This moral life is always born of a religious consciousness, the sense of a higher more ultimate purpose.

So, for example, some people are atheists, they prefer to stay away from the pool, safely inside away from it all. Some are agnostic, they don't really know, but are open or curious, so they sit nearby, beyond the splash zone, keeping dry. Others are cautious believers who enter the waters of religion gradually, now a little in, now a little out. And there are some who, given the witness of others, find themselves immersed, deep into the Good, in the desire for ultimate Goodness that they are aware of the Goodness of existence itself and existence's ultimate good, that is God.

Now some people might hear the word "religion" and miss the point of what the ultimate value of goodness is all about. "To be, or not to be" is the famous and oft quoted line of Shakespeare (1564-1616) from Hamlet (Act III, Scene I), which really is the fundamental moral question of existence. For we all are confronted with the reality of ultimate existence! What lies beyond this life? "The dread of something after death, the undiscovered country from whose bourn no traveler returns" as Hamlet opines. Without the "Moral Imperative" that according to Immanuel Kant (1724-1804) commands us, our desires for the good would be limited to the horizon of this life. It is however the religious consciousness of the Good that allows us to glimpse beyond this life's horizon, the "bourn" from which no traveler returns. It is fitting that we bind ourselves so as to belong to the ultimate good of existence, to our being and becoming good even beyond the limits of our horizon.

Religion, in its most universal sense, is first and foremost about being connected, linked to the foundational reality of life itself. Religion is about belonging. It is this unique consciousness, or awareness of being connected, that is at the heart of all religions. Connected to the earth, connected to the heavens, connected to family and clan, connected to the cosmos. As we explore the bonds that connect us we find that both our head and our heart try to give expression to this primal connection. Religious awareness is first and foremost about belonging and only gradually does it formulate and come to expression in statements and doctrines. The heart longs to name it "beloved." Naming this relational mystery is one of the great challenges. St. Augustine, who did a lot of searching, tells us: "To fall in love with God is the greatest of all romances; to seek Him, the greatest adventure; to find Him, the greatest human achievement." Words may fail, but often signs and symbols, parables and rituals, say more before a word is even spoken. It becomes a struggle when we try to name that which can never fully be named, that is mystery. Religion, rather than being a limiting of life, it is in fact a great freeing so as to be immersed in the flow of life itself. We belong! The more one is grounded and connected to the reality of existence, the stronger is this religious current. Existence, the reality of being, achieves this religious awareness, or consciousness, in the ecstatic. Our experiencing the Mystical Braid of the True, the Beautiful, and the Good bestows and alters the being-ness of life into the delightful and rapturous encounter with absolute mystery that we call God. We cry out, "Thou!" All of creation is not objectified as an it, but we discover the relational mystery of the Creator, like Augustine we "fall in love with God."

The Mystical Braid, in the Good, as we engage it in the moral religious realm, integrates with art and science. These are the disciplines we employ to grasp perfection in its delightfully flawed existence. Religion, or religious consciousness, is always about the vast chasm that exists between where we are and where we are meant to be. One is incapable of the Good without this sense of belonging, which is in fact religious consciousness. Such consciousness frames reality in light of relationships. Our relationship with the Absolute Reality, or God, and with one another. Here is where we see the Good as part of the Mystical Braid working with Science and Art to ground us in existence itself, the being and becoming of life. For the Mystical Braid is One, it is one great relational reality. Truth must always be Beautiful and Good. Beauty must always be Good and True. The Good must always be True and Beautiful. Ernst Cassirer (1874-1945) in *An Essay on Man: An Introduction to a Philosophy of Human Culture* (1944) observed:

> The scientist cannot attain his end without strict obedience to the facts of nature. But this obedience is not passive submission. The work of all the great natural scientists – of Galileo and Newton, of Maxwell and Helmholtz, of Planck and Einstein—was not mere fact collecting; it was theoretical, and that means constructive, work. This spontaneity and productivity is the very center of all human activities. It is man's highest power and it designates at the same time the natural boundary of our human world. In language, in religion, in art, in science, man can do no more than to build up his own universe – a symbolic universe that enables him to understand and interpret, to articulate and organize, to synthesize and universalize his human experience. (221)

While he doesn't speak of the Mystical Braid I believe this passage names the same reality. I believe that Cassirer would appreciate the belonging and the connection we see in the being and becoming of human existence.

The Tyranny of Perfection tries to undo this Mystical Braid and in so doing we are alienated from the being and becoming of life, the depth of our existence. It is our mistrust and suspicion of genuine pleasure that tries to undo the Mystical Braid. When Science, and Art, and Religion are not inter-related, inter-weaving and inter-woven, they no longer connect us with the being-ness and becoming-ness of human existence, which is pleasure in its purest form. It was with the Scientific Revolution, the time of thinkers like Nicolaus Copernicus (1473–1543), Galileo Galilei (1564–1642), and Kepler (1571–1630) that we see a linguistic shift in the concept of pleasure. Up to around the middle of the 16th century "pleasure" largely meant "to take pleasure in," an ecstatic re-location outside oneself. By mid-century it meant "to give pleasure to." No longer grounded in existence but it was reduced to one's personal proprietary realm. And it is in the 17th century that pleasure was taken to have a sexual sense, reducing it even more. This shift from pleasure as our engagement with existence to its being derivative, something we get, is telling. Science was being severed from the Mystical Braid and we see how invention and exploitation, distorted human pleasure in the being and becoming of existence. Art would no longer be seen as expressing Creation and the Creator, but now became a commodity of industry. Religion too, would no longer be seen as connecting the secular to the sacred, but

Chapter Five – "For Goodness Sake..."
47

as a geo-political tool for colonial domination and economic exploitation. Without the interweave of the Mystical Braid, the reality of genuine pleasure is lost and this is most evident in the loss of Religion, the loss of Goodness. Of the Mystical Braid's three strands, the Good is perhaps the most significant! Our engagement of Goodness in Religious Consciousness and in Religion is the most essential in our sense of belonging, of being and becoming connected with existence. There is an old saying that I think is appropriate: "Good people are like candles; they burn themselves up to give others light." The Tyranny of Perfection has exploited Science to see perfection as a derivative, a pleasure given to me. Whereas Perfectibility or True Perfection is found in the Mystical Braid of Truth, Beauty, and Goodness that connect us to the being and becoming of life. Science, Art and Religion are our engagement of the Mystical Braid and enable us to discover the True, the Beautiful, and the Good, which is our delight in belonging. Religion is about being Good for goodness sake, and that bestows on us the greatest sense of belonging. The truly perfect comes at the end, the beautifully perfect comes with the pleasure of being and becoming, and the goodly perfect comes with belonging, being good for goodness sake!

Chapter VI

"Just Right" – On True Perfection

So what are we struggling with when we encounter the tyranny of perfection? In short it is an issue of virtue. Let's take a brief look at the much loved children's story of "Goldilocks and the Three Bears." There are multiple versions but the one I recall from my childhood involved a young girl wandering in the woods who came upon the house of three bears -- the Papa Bear, the Mama Bear and Baby Bear. For the sake of brevity, the girl moves from one chair to the other, to each bowl of porridge, to each of the beds, each time preferring that option which wasn't the extreme, but was, in her words, "just right." I mentioned this in chapter one, and it has become known as the "Goldilocks Principle." It is the ability to find the happy mean between the extremes, where genuine perfection, as being complete, is to be found.

In this children's tale we are given a valuable life lesson about balance. The ancient thinkers spoke of this as virtue. Aristotle and Thomas Aquinas both saw virtue as core to the perfectibility of a person. It is the benevolent side of what perfectibility is meant to be. Virtues are the "just rightness" of life that lead us to our ultimate end. So why do we need these guides? To answer that question, we need to examine the underlying doubt that has destroyed our pleasure in life. Recall Freud's concept of the Pleasure Principle (*Lustprinzip*). According to it, humans instinctively seek pleasure and avoid pain. The problem, I see, arises when we realize that human growth and flourishing, at times, must avoid pleasure and endure the pain (e.g. childbirth, physical therapy, study).

The Mystical Braid, the transcendental of Truth, Beauty, Goodness, opens to us the means to connect to the being and becoming of life, to existence itself. It is the pleasant flow of life that science, art, and religion probe and ponder. This is why Freud's "Pleasure Principle" can so easily undermine the genuine delight of perfectibility, the becoming of being. Suspicion, doubt, and mistrust of science, art, religion, and one for the other, seek to undo the Mystical Braid that connects us to existence. This suspicious mistrust of pleasure is the most self-alienating deception, for it robs us of the sensual and sexual incarnate reality which are meant to draw us into the *torrens vita*, the flood waters of life. If we try to "unbraid" the Mystical Braid, the dynamic interplay becomes fractured, the chord is weakened.

Allow me to explain. The Renaissance artist Michelangelo has a beautifully breath-taking sculpting of the Risen Christ that stands in the Dominican Church of Santa Maria supra Minerva. In it we can see the dynamic interplay of what science, art, and religion are meant to be. Science or craft has trusted in the mathematical and technical skill to work the marble slab into a sensual and sexual human form, almost life-like, lacking only an animate soul. Michelangelo has captured the Truth of the human form. The naked form captures the male body and

Michelangelo, as can be seen in the original version, displays the Risen Lord's sexual organs, purely, naturally, innocently. The Risen Lord holds the cross, the instrument of his bodily torment. The death-shroud has fallen behind him, his right leg and right arm serpentine around the cross, as if to mock the serpent of the Fall and the Rod of Asclepius, declaring Christ alone is the true physician. His torso is turned, looking caringly to his left, staring down the sinister side toward the doubt and mistrust of sin and death. His arms cradle the cross of hope, of redemption, of salvation. Originally Michelangelo sculpted the body without wounds (which others later added) and it was in the Baroque period that a bronze loincloth was added for modesty's sake. The Truth and Beauty and Goodness so masterfully captured in Michelangelo's original sculpting did not give in to the mistrust of the physical, the sensual, the sexual, that plagued a later age. Rather in Michelangelo's *Risen Christ*, delight and pleasure are trusted in the intertwining of science, and art, and religion.

If I might say a few words on how this triad of the Mystical Braid affords us a sense of true perfection and genuine pleasure in life. Only by seeing the inter-relatedness of science, art, and religion are we able to appreciate their distinct contribution and their common character. **Science**, in its relation to the True, confronts the base realities of our world-context. It is the most fundamental encounter with reality and our efforts to relate to reality. Science in its primitive form is the child grabbing and groping at the world, hoping to understand all the experiences of life. Fundamentally science is about our sense of security, our understanding the world around us and how to relate to it and with it. If our world were only so one dimensional it would be a very grey and flat reality, a puzzle without promise.

Art, in its pursuit of the Beautiful, brings texture and color into one's world. Here is where the pleasures of sight, sound, taste, touch, and smell awaken in us delight, desire, and longing. Without this bridge between the facts of our world, the empirical and mundane given-ness of things, life would be without pleasure. For it is in Art that we are seduced by the object we call beautiful, because it fetches us and lures our imagination beyond. As children, and the child in us all, have often looked up at the clouds passing overhead and observed them. We know what they are. But then, as we watch with no real deliberation they seem to take the shape of a face, another that of an animal or another that of an object. Feelings stir within and we find our innermost self, becoming connected to the object or thing in a different fashion, and then it dissipates. A stone or mountain range, with permanence, can appear to be something more, possibly a ship, or a turtle, or a castle. Our imagination wonders at its origin, and its relationship to us now takes on added meaning. Lore and legend, story and imagination, paint a picture of ancient times, of long lost civilizations, of our ancestors and our future. It is this reality of Beauty that brings the Truth of Science to the threshold of Religion, in its inspiring vision of the Good, its quest of ultimate meaning.

It is **Religion** that lifts the veil beyond the physical order and explores the metaphysical realm. Religion is about belonging and as it explores the Good, Religion engages the Absolute and the Ultimate. Awe and Wonder are the proper stance of Religion, for by opening us up to an ultimate belonging, to a sense that we are part of something more, we come full circle. By that I mean Religion bends back upon itself to engage both Science and Art, both Truth and Beauty, in order to make sense of the limitless wonder. Saint Anselm of Canterbury (1033–1109) spoke of this link of the Good back to the True, of Religion reaching back into Science when he described theology, saying it is "faith seeking understanding" (*fides quaerens intellectum*). Religion engages Science with a new fascination beyond the physical order – the metaphysics of existence! British philosopher of science John Dupré tells us: "When we first pull a fish out of the sea, we might wisely remain agnostic about how such an unusual entity got to be there. After thousands of fish of many different kinds, we are entitled to infer that there is a whole strange, living world down there under the waves. Similarly, since science aims to discover truths about the world, surely it should tell us something about the very deepest levels of our reality, which is to say, metaphysics."[7]

---

[7] John Dupré, "Metaphysics of Metamorphosis" in <u>Aeon</u> edited by Sally Davies (https://aeon.co/essays/science-and-metaphysics-must-work-together-to-answer-lifes-deepest-questions - 5/22/2019). Dupré wrote *Processes of Life: Essays in the Philosophy of Biology* (2012); and *The Disorder of Things: Metaphysical Foundations of the Disunity of Science* (1995)

Chapter Six – "Just Right" – On True Perfection

The Mystical Braid is the interplay of Science, Art, and Religion. Logic, aesthetics, and ethics are deeply linked together and the cosmos encounters itself in Truth, Beauty, and Goodness, the mysterious revelation of God. It is the inter-relatedness of things that moves beyond the suspicion of pleasure, especially physical pleasure, but delights in discovery. I need to repeat that, The Mystical Braid is the interplay of Science, Art, and Religion. Logic, aesthetics, and ethics are deeply linked together and the cosmos encounters itself in Truth, Beauty, and Goodness, the mysterious revelation of God.

A hermeneutics that stirs up our suspicion and doubt about the physical, sensual and sexual human flourishing wears down our ability to see the worlds profound relatedness. This relatedness is both the agony and the ecstasy of life. The Tyranny of Perfection denies the painful reality of struggle, brokenness and the challenges that bring forth deep and abiding pleasure. Any athlete or artist knows the paradoxical link between effort, struggle, endurance, on the one hand, and growth, satisfaction, achievement, on the other. When it comes to the ultimate aim of life, it is our knowing, appreciating, and believing that makes life meaningful. In his *De Regimine Principum* (*On the Government of Rulers*) chapter VI, St. Thomas Aquinas suggests three ways of avoiding the evil of a tyrant that can instruct us. Simply put they are: the proper character of a person not to be a tyrant; the lack of opportunity to behave like a tyrant; and restrictions on tyrannical behavior. Now the perfectionism that I have been talking about isn't a person but more our own personality type, we might say. So how do we tame the tyrant within? I think Thomas offers some helpful considerations. It is the virtue found in a person, in the society in which we live, and in the actions we undertake. So if we try to tame our perfectionism, if we try to learn to take true pleasure in life, we will need to address these three things: character, opportunity, and behavior. We do this, as we have said, by finding the "just right" balance in life and that we call Virtue.

Chapter Six – "Just Right" – On True Perfection

Chapter VII

"Love Makes the World Go Round"

In classical thought virtues enable a person to live morally by their acquired habit of the Good. The virtue tailor-made for combating our suspicion of pleasure and our misconception of perfection is the virtue of love (*caritas*) or charity. This love is a selfless love as opposed to the passionate love of *eros* or the obsessive love of *mania*. *Caritas* or *agape* is that self-less love for all. As St. Paul so beautifully wrote: "Love is patient; love is kind; love is not envious or boastful or arrogant or rude. It does not insist on its own way; it is not irritable or resentful; it does not rejoice in wrongdoing, but rejoices in the truth. It bears all things, believes all things, hopes all things, endures all things. Love never ends...." (I Cor. 13:4-8)[8] So how does the virtue of self-less love restore trust in human pleasure and human perfectibility? It does it by calling us back from the edge of self-destruction to realize life's meaning which is a remarkable relational wonder, a mix of good and bad, of being and becoming.

Allow me to explain. Lili, in the 1961 Broadway musical *Carnival*, is an orphaned young girl who looks hopefully for a job in the carnival. Instead she experiences betrayal, ridicule and unhappiness. Paul, who unhappily works in the carnival, and had been crippled in war, once had dreams of

---

[8] https://www.biblegateway.com/passage/?search=I+cor+13&version=NRSVCE 5/23/2019

being a dancer, but now works as a so-so puppeteer. In Lili's despair she climbs the trapeze ladder with the intent of jumping to her death. As she ascends she hears a voice, that of one of the puppets speaking to her. Lili fails to realize who the puppeteer is and Paul is unable to open up to her, so he speaks through his puppets. Lili is brought back from her self-destructive mission and she sings a comforting song to one of the puppets: "Love makes the world go 'round / Love makes the world go 'round / Somebody soon will love you / If no one loves you now. / High in some silent sky / Love sings a silver song / Making the Earth whirl softly / Love makes the world go 'round."[9] While Lili forsakes her plan, she remains in the carnival but love is not so easily found. She faces deception, physical abuse, and humiliation. Paul hides behind a façade of harshness and cruelty toward Lili who comes to hate him, even though she unknowingly finds love's tenderness through Paul's four little puppets. However, confronted by a co-worker, Paul realizes that he has made Lili believe the world is a cruel and loveless place. After a mishap Lili is fired from the carnival and plans to leave. She encounters two of the puppets who ask her to take them with her. In their exchange Paul is revealed as the puppeteer and Lili realizes another side of Paul, who now risks confessing his love for her. As complicated as love may be, as difficult and as painful, it is the fundamental motivating reality.

---

[9]

https://lyricsplayground.com/alpha/songs/l/lovemakestheworldgoround patboone.html 5/23/2019

Chapter Seven – "Love Makes the World Go Round"

Love does move us, and it does "make the world go round."

But what does this musical teach us? Both Lili and Paul were held captive by a false sense of perfection. Lili hoped the carnival would be her new life, "a little girl's dream." It was to be her new moment and new promise, which was not the reality. Paul, perhaps more tragically, was weighed down by his perception that his injury left him imperfect, incomplete, less a person, not appreciated, a person in search of a reason to be. In fact one of his song's is just about that: "I've got to find a reason / For living on this earth / Something to want / Something to be / Somehow to say / I am me."[10] The fact is that both Lili and Paul mistrust the reality of their life which they deemed imperfect. It was through the intermediary of the puppets that each could and would learn to trust the flawed reality of life. The song Lili first sang to the puppets presents a haunting tender Beauty, the Truth of Lili's and Paul's loneliness is accepted and acknowledged, and the fundamental, if not buried Good in each person, enables each to trust. The imperfection of life is not an obstacle to enjoyment, it does not prevent us from taking genuine delight in the reality of one another. For we all have a broken bit in us and often times that is our deepest beauty, our greatest good, our most redeeming truth. More often than not we love another not because they are perfect but because we see the good amid their brokenness.

---

[10] https://www.allmusicals.com/lyrics/carnival/ivegottofindareason.htm 5/23/2019

Chapter Seven – "Love Makes the World Go Round"

Love (*caritas*) is the antidote to our repressive Freudian deception that we are meant to be perfect and that our passions, our drives, our sensuality and sexuality are base things, beneath our humanity. Rather, it is exactly in our struggle with them that we encounter a fuller sense of self and our relationship with one another and with the world. It seems the more we try to suppress our most natural self, the more destruction we do. In psychology we see this in what is called socialization, how a person is formed from early on into adulthood. It provides the most fundamental sense of a person's belonging. It is how a person internalizes the social reality, norms, values, and culture. A repressive socialization lacks freedom, and a permissive socialization lacks direction.

But what do we mean by freedom? This is critical today when we are preoccupied with individual personal freedom and end up with division and enmity in society. Freedom always fails if it is selfish and self-centered! Fundamentally freedom must be about relationship, association, belonging. In John's gospel Jesus offers his disciples this simple revelation, "If you continue in my word, you are truly my disciples; and you will know the truth, and the truth will make you free" (John 8:31-32 NRSVCE). Freedom is *de facto* a relational reality and requires us to engage our world, our neighbors, and yes, even our enemies to discover what is true. Freedom is not a "freedom from" but a "freedom for" which engages the Other. Isolation, alienation, division are not true freedom! "Leave me alone" is the motto of a self-imposed jail sentence. True freedom demands a relationship that bestows knowledge about the ultimate reality, that is God. In the phrase "truly my disciple," the Greek text uses the disclosive and revealing sense of truth in *aletheia* and the word "disciple" carries a sense of being students of the Incarnate Mystery of God (ἀληθῶς μαθηταί). Jesus puts it in a much more personal way when he says "you are of me" (μού ἐστε). In the first part of the passage, the word translated here as "continue" also has a deeper sense and that is "to abide" (μείνητε). John uses it one other time when Jesus speaks of the true vine, "If you abide in me, and my words abide in you…" (John 15:7 NRSVCE). We have made the fatal mistake of equating freedom with a legal status, a kind of entitlement under the law. To do so reduces our freedom to a mere social norm, a legal standing, and denies freedom the intimacy of a real personal relationship with the Creator of the cosmos, our encounter with God. Our freedom is to engage the world and one another. Our failure to do so shifts freedom to a controlling repressive norm of law, subordinating human relationship to legalities and litigation. Jesus, unlike Aristotle, saw the moral life as ultimately a relationship with the Father. Aquinas developed Jesus' teaching on our living relationally with God. As much as reason can help us to navigate the moral seas of life it is only in our relationship to a caring and compassionate God that we find the safe harbor at life's end.

So we are free to love, not selfishly or self-centeredly, but to love relationally (*caritas*). Any dissension or division that ruptures the profound sense of belonging to and with one another and our world undermines this selfless love.

Chapter Seven – "Love Makes the World Go Round"

With that said, this selfless love doesn't demand conformity or even agreement, rather it finds pleasure in the difference. For far too long the Tyranny of Perfection has corrupted the "Harmony of Difference," a *kata holos* or "catholic" way of thinking, that is a holistic way of living. The Tyranny of Perfection failed to understand this relational love, which after all, is the mystery of the Trinity. We see it at work in conflicts of the early Church, and in the disputes that arose between Jewish believers and Gentile converts. It sought to undermine the fundamental unity in Christ with religious wars, with its effort to corrupt the ministry of Christ in a lust for political power and prestige. Even today it divides the Church with a false notion of perfection and a failure to forgive. Relational love endures even with the brokenness, the weakness, and flawed reality of life because relational love is for the weak, the lost, the destitute, the sinner. In the story of "Carnival" Lili and Paul learned the lesson of relational love—we are all a bit broken and forgiveness is the fix, mercy is the medicine.

Chapter VIII
Conclusion: Taming the Tyrant

As we have explored the tyranny of perfection, our failure to live with flaws, we might ask as to what its opposite would be. What is the opposite of the tyranny of perfection? In so doing we glimpse a new perspective on the question. The answer it seems to me would be, the benevolence of imperfection! This points us in the direction that love knows only so well. In seeing the imperfection as something that wills a good, it becomes a blessing that is conceived and in time will come to birth. So how might we tame the tyrant?

First off, we must see that the emperor has no clothes, as the children's story teaches. The Freudian mistrust of pleasure and delight that has been pathologically reduced to sexual dysfunction begins to poison all good and valuable pleasure, all genuine delight. We must begin to trust once more the beauty of conjugal love, its fullest meaning found in the sacred bond that brings forth life and love. To do so takes nothing away from the deep and abiding love felt for others, but it does cherish and delight in this unique source of life and family. We know too, that the unitive bond of love deprived of conjugal love is not without its delight, its familial love. By adoption we discover the love not born but bestowed. Baptism is such an adoption wherein we are made sons and daughters of our God, brothers and sisters in Christ and co-heirs to the Kingdom of God (Romans 8:16-17). As imperfect as we are in living the Christian life, it takes nothing away from our birthright. Sin and imperfection are not the issue. The tragedy unfolds when we allow the sin, the flaw, to alienate us from one another and from God. A wise person once said that it doesn't matter how many times you fall and sin, what matters is your getting back up and trying again. Sadly, the tyranny of perfection cannot permit the frailty and brokenness of humanity to be. The tyrant's downfall is the unmerited mercy of a loving God!

Jesus so often taught that the imperfect, the sinners, the weak who know their flaws, their failings, are often closer to God than are the self-righteous. The Samaritans, both the woman at the well (John 4:1-42) and the traveler who cared for a stranger (Luke 10:25-37); tax collectors (Luke 18:9-14); prostitutes (Matthew 21:31-32); sinners (Luke 15:2) all found the "benevolence of imperfection," the meaning of mercy shown to the vulnerable and broken. St. Therese of Lisieux, who lived during the time of Freud, offers us just such a spirituality of trust, calling it "the way of simple loving trust," or the "way of trust and love."[11] She learned to trust the Lord's generosity with our limitations and in her autobiography, she wrote: "…for I am too little to climb up the steep stairway of perfection" (*Story of a Soul*, IX). She discovered what St. Paul too discovered, "for whenever I am weak, then I am strong" (2

---

[11] The French author Jacques Phillippe used this phrase from St. Therese in his inspiring 2012 work *The Way of Trust and Love. A Retreat Guided by St. Therese of Lisieux* (Scepter Publisher).

Chapter Eight – Conclusion: Taming the Tyrant

Corinthians 12:10). But why have so many of us failed to understand this today?

Mistrust! That says it all. Sadly, we have forgotten the importance of trust and our fixation on perfection tricks us into thinking that one must be flawless to be trustworthy. Trustworthiness is about faithfulness and not flawlessness, it is the "way of simple loving trust" that Therese knew. So many young people, in part due to a false idealism, get it wrong. There is a grotesque and vile tendency to create mistrust, to so focus on the little imperfections or even greater failings of a person and discredit them, lose all faith in others, and ultimately lose our faith in humanity and faith in God. Our inability to risk, to be vulnerable, keeps us from discovering the benevolent side of imperfection. Instead we build up barriers, create defense mechanisms, play games that insulate us from the very realities of life that must be encountered. Freudian suspicion of human sexuality, the genders' mistrust of one another, our profound doubt about human reproduction, and even society's exploitation of sex, have all created an obstacle to human delight and wonder, to frailty and fidelity in life itself.

Freudian mistrust is best confronted in those things that most connect us to the fundamental ground of our being and becoming, that Mystical Braid of Truth, Beauty, and Goodness. Only in trusting the inner-connectedness of these three transcendental strands will tyranny give way to benevolence and perfection discover imperfection's worth. The tyrant is tamed by our honestly, creatively and faithfully exploring the braid of the ultimate values discovered in science, art, and religion. I fear that many of our universities have failed us in that they have compartmentalized, departmentalized, even segregated these three disciplines. They have created specialized silos in independent fields at odds and at war with one another. We need the poets and artists to help us bridge these three, but more, we need every scientist, artist, and theologian to engage the blend of their special call. Why? Because they have each been entrusted with a social-making task of truth-naming, beauty-seeing, and faith-trusting that grounds our fragile human project. Let me explain. The mountains where I live are a remarkable mix of geological formation, artistic beauty, and inspiring faith. However, each alone is inadequate. Separated, each fails to capture the inter-related meaning, not only of the scientist, the artist or the theologian, but more so, of the community, that social bond in which they all live. If science has no beauty or inspiration, if art has no truth or holiness, if religion has no inquiry or pleasure, they fail to serve their purpose. Albert Einstein, Michelangelo, and Augustine were arguing in heaven as to who was right. Mary happened upon them and asked why they were so excited. They told her what each one was arguing. Einstein said "energy" best names God, Michelangelo said "color" best names God, and Augustine said "spirit" best names God. Frustrated they turned to Mary. She looked at them and said one word – "be" which echoed in each man's heart as they heard: be-come, be-hold, be-lieve.

Chapter Eight – Conclusion: Taming the Tyrant

Science, art, and religion share in the discovery, the unfolding, and the finding of life. The trick is to trust that each in its own way bestows a richer and fuller blessing to us all. Ernest Hemingway once said, "The best way to find out if you can trust somebody is to trust them." There is a pearl found in this simple statement. Trust is the only way to open ourselves up to the deep and meaningful relations we all desire. Suspicion and mistrust do more to imprison one's soul. Trust is the only way to be free. The tyranny of perfection is a self-imposed confinement which cannot trust the broken bit in us all, which fails to find the world trustworthy and fails to see its truth, its beauty, and its goodness.

Acknowledgements

This project has been born of the many stories I heard from people who feel so frustrated, so disappointed, and so discouraged with where things seem to be today. But even more, the great tragedy is that many of them have come to mistrust the very thing that will most redeem their world, a religious sense of life. I am grateful to the number of young millennials who have time and time again expressed their disbelief in belief. Or, by the same token millennials who time and time again are mad at my generation for what they think we got wrong in religion, politics, in short life. Had it not been for their alarm, it would never have occurred to me that they are suffering from the same thing, a crisis of trust. I am grateful to the number of people who have boiled with anger over the scandals in the Church and who have been plagued by a crisis of faith, to believe beyond what is apparent. Strangely, I am also grateful for the deaths of those I have loved and the challenge, the inexplicable challenge of finality. I am grateful because in a culture of mistrust, anger, despair, and loss we have been brought to an awakening. It will take time for us to realize that the agony of what is hurting us can only be healed by our learning to struggle together, to trust the hurt, and to risk our vulnerabilities.

I would like to thank those women and men who have shared with me their life's journey over the years and who have helped me to discover that the true perfection of life is found in the cracks and flaws of life. I am indebted to the individuals who generously took time to read over this manuscript and offer comments and insight. This work is by no means perfect. No doubt, as there always seems to be, there remain many flaws that better editing might have fixed, better phrasing might have clarified, or better examples may have spoken more beautifully. But, in a book about the tyranny of perfection, imperfections are in fact a welcomed reminder. To those who took the time to read my drafts and share their comments I am grateful for the two-fold risk we have shared. Honesty is not an easy thing but it is always appreciated. I especially wish to acknowledge: Joan See whose helpful reading and thoughtful questions contributed greatly to the final draft; Joseph Bailham for his encouragement and insights into his generation; Gary Braun for his doggedly tenacious questions; Vanessa Guerin for helping me see connections with other hidden perspectives; Nick Monco for his clarifications, and Timothy Combs for references to some valuable authors. I am also thankful for the time and opportunity I have been given by the Archdiocese of Santa Fe and Archbishop John C. Wester who allowed me to work remotely for a month, and to the Dominican Order for a tradition of making sense out of life. I am grateful to the Dominicans at Blackfriars in Oxford for their hospitality and academic resources. And finally, a word of thanks to my readers, for your curiosity and interest. Readers and reading remain a critical variable in a meaningful life and a good society. As St. Thomas Aquinas reportedly said, "I fear the person of just one book" (*hominem unius libri timeo*).

Acknowledgements

Desert Willow Project

The Desert Willow Project is a pilot program in author independence, fostering greater editorial self-determination and freer creative choices. The project is named for Desert Willow, a resilient shrub native to the Southwest. It is known for its ability to survive in extreme climates, and still, it blooms with willowy leaves and beautiful flowers, even given difficult circumstances. Not unlike many independent authors, who face extreme challenges, yet their creativity still produces exceptional talent. Opportunities in self-publishing now provide ways for these authors to reach more readers. The DWP promotes the value of independent writers to produce and publish, free from the conventional media industry. DWP authors are also members of the Independent Author Network (IAN), a community of authors who are self-published or published by a small indie press.

DesertWillowProjectUSA@gmail.com

About the Author

Michael Thomas-Paul Demkovich, (1954-) a Dominican Friar who has written on Spirituality, Theology and Meister Eckhart in journals and books. He holds a Ph.D. and the Pontifical Doctorate, both from the Katholiek Universiteit Leuven. From 1991 to 1996 he taught in St. Louis, MO before becoming the Founding Director of the Dominican Ecclesial Institute (Albuquerque, NM). In 2009 he was named the Gerald Vann Visiting Fellow at Blackfriars, Oxford. He served as President of the International Dominican Foundation and is currently serving in the Archdiocese of Santa Fe as the Episcopal Vicar for Doctrine and Life.

Other Works by This Author

"Work as Worth, Money or Meaning" in *Connections Between Spirit and Work in Career Development* (1997)

Introducing Meister Eckhart (2006)

A Soul-Centered Life (2010).

The Death of Magister Aycardus (2011)

We Walk By Faith (2018)

www.ingramcontent.com/pod-product-compliance
Lightning Source LLC
Chambersburg PA
CBHW051737040426
42447CB00008B/1180